Green Line
5

von
Victoria Clark
Carolyn Jones
Anja Treinies

herausgegeben von
Harald Weisshaar

Ernst Klett Verlag
Stuttgart · Leipzig

Hallo liebe Schülerinnen und Schüler,

mit Green Line 5 Vokabeltraining aktiv kannst du die neuen Vokabeln aus deinem Englischbuch üben.

Es ist immer gut, neue Wörter in einem Satz zu lernen. Du findest daher zu jeder Seite in deinem Schulbuch unter „What do you remember?" englische Sätze, die du am besten mit Bleistift vervollständigen kannst. Dabei helfen dir auf der linken Seite deutsche Sätze mit den dick gedruckten Lernwörtern aus deinem Buch, deren englische Entsprechungen du rechts in die Lücken der englischen Sätze eintragen sollst. Manchmal gibt es aber auch statt der Sätze Bilder als Hinweis darauf, was in die Lücke gehört.

Hier zwei Beispiele:

Ich mag keine **Prüfungen**.	I don't like _____ .
Ich würde ein **Praktikum** als vorziehen.	I would prefer _____ as a _____ .

Deine Lösungen kannst du auf den Seiten 58–64 selbst überprüfen. Achte dabei auch auf die korrekte Schreibung der Wörter. Hast du dich an die richtigen Wörter erinnert und sie fehlerfrei geschrieben, kannst du in die Kästchen am Rand ein Häkchen setzen.

Notiere die Wörter, bei denen du Schwierigkeiten hattest, und lerne sie noch einmal. Du kannst z. B. Karteikarten mit den Wörtern anlegen und damit üben. Versuche dann erneut, die Sätze zu vervollständigen.

Wenn du alle Kästchen abhaken kannst, beherrschst du alle wichtigen Wörter dieser Seite, du hast also deine Vokabeln gut gelernt. Du kannst außerdem versuchen, die englischen Übungssätze links zuzuhalten und die deutschen selbst zu übersetzen. So kannst du alles noch einmal wiederholen und festigen.

Zusätzlich gibt es noch viele Rätsel und andere spannende Aufgaben für dich, damit du die neuen Wörter üben und ausprobieren kannst. Diese findest du immer unten auf jeder Seite.

Viel Spaß und Erfolg mit deinem Vokabeltraining aktiv!

Inhaltsverzeichnis

Zoom-in	3
Unit 1	9
Unit 2	16
Revision Unit 1+2	30
Unit 3	31
Unit 4	39
Revision Unit 3+4	57
Lösungen	58

Zoom-in The world speaks English

→ pages 8–11

What do you remember?

Der australische **Kontinent** hat eine **einzigartige** Tierwelt.	The Australian _____ has got a _____ animal world.
	The Australians call this animal a _____ . We call it a _____ .
Koalas und **Schnabeltiere** leben in (*Spitzname für Australien*).	_____ and _____ live _____ .
Die **Aborigines** sind eine **Minderheit** in der australischen **Gesellschaft**.	The _____ are a _____ in Australian _____ .
Sie sind die **einheimische** Bevölkerung Australiens.	They are the _____ population of Australia.
Ihre Heimat ist das **australische Hinterland**.	Their home is the _____ .
Es gibt viele **getrennte Aborigine**familien.	There are many _____ families.
Das ist das Ergebnis **erzwungener Umsiedlung**.	This is the result of _____ .

1 Mixed bag

Fill in the missing words.

indigenous   forced relocation   unique   koalas
separated   Aboriginal   outback   kangaroos   Aborigines   continent

1. The Australian _____ is a huge area. It is the home of the _____ people of Australia – the _____ .

2. _____ families were torn apart by _____ .

3. Australia has been a _____ for 50 million years, _____ from the rest of the world. That's why _____ animals live there. _____ and _____ , for example.

three **3**

Z Zoom-in

→ pages 8–11

What do you remember?

Die **Australier** *(ugs.)* sagen manchmal … um sich zu begrüßen.	The __Aussies__ sometimes say '__G'day__ (= __Good day__ !)' to say hello.
Die **Weite** des **Regenwaldes** ist atemberaubend.	The __radius__ of the __Rainforest__ is breathtaking.
Teile der **Ozonschicht** über Australien sind **zerstört**.	Parts of the __ozone layer__ above Australia are __destroyed__.
Deswegen bekommen viele Leute **Hautkrebs**.	That's why many people get __skin cancer__.
Wälder und **Tundra** sind Teil der **kanadischen** Landschaft.	__Forests__ and __tundra__ are part of the __canadian__ landscape.
Die britische **Monarchin** ist Kanadas **Staatsoberhaupt**.	The British __monarchi__ is Canada's __Präsident__.
	Her __head__ is on the money.

2 Landscapes

Complete the crossword puzzle and find the solution.

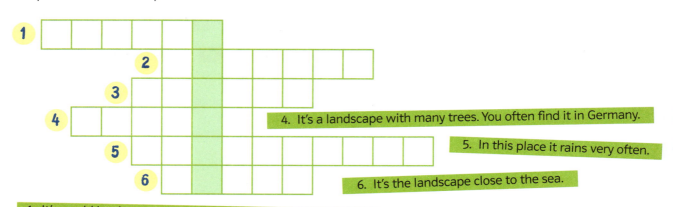

4. It's a landscape with many trees. You often find it in Germany.
5. In this place it rains very often.
6. It's the landscape close to the sea.
1. It's a cold landscape without any trees. You find it in Canada, for example.
3. This area is very dry. You find it in Africa and Australia, for example.
2. It's a huge area in Australia where you can drive for days without meeting anybody.

Solution: Casually, an Australian can be called an _____ .

4 four

Zoom-in Z

→ pages 8–11

What do you remember?

Die französische Sprache hat einen **dominierenden Status** in Frankreich.	The French language has got a _dominating_ _status_ in France.	☐
Es gibt dort eine **systematische Regelung** der Sprache.	There is a _systematic regulation_ of language.	☐
Das Ziel ist es, keine **Fremd**wörter zu benutzen.	The goal is not to use any _feature_ words.	☐
Sie wollen den **Einfluss** der englischen Sprache nicht akzeptieren.	They don't want to accept the _influense_ of the English language.	☐
Aber Englisch ist auch die Sprache der **Popkultur**.	But English is also the language of _popkultur_.	☐
Sie wurde immer wichtiger, als Amerika zu einer **Supermacht** aufstieg.	It became more and more important when America became a _superpower_.	☐
Amerikanische Technologie **führte** zu einem weltweiten Gebrauch von Englisch.	American technology _led_ to a worldwide use of English.	☐

3 English words in German

Write down five words of English origin you use in your normal language.

_____
_____

4 Your opinion

What do you think about the French way of dealing with foreign languages? Should we try not to use foreign words? In a few sentences, write down your opinion and give reasons for it. Use at least five of the given words.

`influence` `superpower` `to destroy` `regulation` `society` `to lead`
`foreign` `status` `unique` `pop culture` `forced` `to dominate`

_____
_____
_____
_____

five

Zoom-in

→ page 8–11

What do you remember?

In Indien gibt es viele **Dialekte**.	In India there are many _____.
Deutschland ist eine **Demokratie**.	Germany is a _____.
Das bedeutet, dass man die **Möglichkeit** hat zu wählen.	That means you have the _____ to elect.
Es gibt **Wahlen** und **Bürgerrechte**.	There are _____ and _____.
Viele Menschen haben Angst vor **Krebs**.	Many people are scared of _____.
Armut ist ein großes Problem für die **indische** Bevölkerung.	_____ is a big problem for the _____ population.
Das britische Reich **löste sich auf**, weil viele Kolonien ihre **Unabhängigkeit** erklärten.	The British Empire _____ because many of the colonies declared their _____.
Amy hat ein gutes **Verhältnis** zu ihrer Familie.	Amy has good _____ with her family.

5 Find the missing word

1. Australia • down under   Australian • _____
2. America • Indians   Australia • _____
3. polar bear • Alaska   koala • _____
4. country • region   language • _____
5. Germany • Europe   country • _____

6 Spot the mistakes

Find two mistakes in every sentence. Underline them and write down the correct version on the lines.

1. Free elections and zivil rights are parts of a democraty.

   _____

2. Australia is also called 'deep under' and 'T'day' is an Australian way to say 'hello'.

   _____

Zoom-in

→ pages 8–11

What do you remember?

Pizza ist ein italienisches **Gericht**.	Pizza is an Italian _____.
Eine **Umfrage** ergab, dass die Menschen den neuen **Präsidenten** mögen.	A _____ said that people like the new _____.
Meine Familie wurde vom Krieg **auseinander gerissen**.	My family was _____ by the war.
In Indien wird **Hindi** gesprochen.	_____ is spoken in India.
Die **Siedlung** ist drei **Quadrat**kilometer groß.	The _____ is three _____ (= _____) km big.
Guten Tag! / Guten Tag!	Indian: "_____!" South African: "_____!"
Ich brauche keine **Erinnerung** um zu wissen, was zu tun ist!	I don't need a _____ to know what to do!
Lasst uns einen **Bollywood**-Film ansehen!	Let's watch a _____ movie!

7 Word formation

Form the words in brackets.

1. India → (adjective)   __Indian__
2. social → (noun)   _____
3. Canada → (adjective)   _____
4. endlessness → (adjective)   _____
5. settler → (noun)   _____
6. reminder → (verb)   _____
7. regular → (noun)   _____
8. leader → (verb)   _____
9. possible → (noun)   _____
10. poverty → (adjective)   _____

8 Bits and pieces

Form words from the syllables and write them down.

| por- | -vey | -rest | -trait |
| fo- | tun- | de- | -cer | out- | -dra | -clare | can- | sta- | sur- | -back | -tus |

_____ _____ _____ _____

_____ _____ _____ _____

Zoom-in

→ pages 8–11

What do you remember?

Dies ist die letzte **Bestellung**, bevor der Pub schließt.	This is the last _____ before the pub closes.
Es ist hier drinnen so **überfüllt**!	It's really _____ in here!
In der gestrigen Radiosendung **rief** ein **Bankier an**.	In yesterday's radio show a _____ _____.
Wir brauchen einen neuen **Anführer** für unsere Fußballmannschaft.	We need a new _____ for our football team.
Könntest du den Film für mich **aufnehmen**?	Could you _____ the movie for me?
Die **Apartheid** war ein **rassistisches System**.	_____ was a _____ _____.
Sie bedeutete **Getrenntheit** von **Schwarzen** und Weißen.	It meant _____ of _____ and white people.
Südafrika war ein **Polizeistaat**.	South Africa was a _____.
Schwarze lebten in **Townships**.	Black people lived in _____.
Jetzt wächst eine schwarze **Mittelklasse** mit mehr **Wohlstand** heran.	Now a black _____ with more _____ is growing.

9 Jumbled words

Put the letters into the right order and match the words with the country they belong to.

TZIWHO   NARTUD   WOLLYBODO   LABOGIRIAN   PSIWOTNH
DARTAHIEP   HIIDN   OCKUTBA   CHRENF   ORO

India	
Canada	
South Africa	
Australia	

Unit 1 Australia

→ pages 12–15

What do you remember?	
Charakterisierung	In order to write a _____ you have to look at how the characters feel and behave.
Atem	Maybe they are shy and scared and hold their _____ when something unusual happens.
selbstsicher • direkt	They might also be _____ and _____ .
adaptiert • gekürzt	Even if stories for students are often _____ and _____ , you can find out a lot about the characters if you look at their actions.

1 Aboriginal life

Find five words/phrases in the box that have to do with Aboriginal life, culture and problems and make a sentence with each.

> the outback • breath • forced relocation • apartheid • Bollywood • British settlement • unique culture • life in townships • direct characterization • natural lifestyle • pop culture • to dominate • abridged • minority • monarch • separated families • systematic killing

1. _____
2. _____
3. _____
4. _____
5. _____

2 Describing a character

Find the right adjective to describe these people.

Adjectives: direct, racist, aggressive, helpful, confident

1. Someone who often does something for other people. → _____
2. A person that often fights with other people. → _____
3. Someone who openly talks about problems. → _____
4. Someone who believes in herself/himself. → _____
5. A person who doesn't like foreign people. → _____

1 Skills

→ page 16

What do you remember?

Lasst uns einen anderen **Standpunkt** betrachten.	Let's look at a different _____.
Stonehenge ist eine **Welterbestätte**.	Stonehenge is a _____.
Diese Notizen sind in **Kurzschrift** geschrieben.	These notes are written in _____.
Interessiert dich das Great Barrier Reef?	Does the Great Barrier Reef _____ you?
Wir könnten eine Tour mit dem **Glasboden**boot machen!	We could go on a _____ boat tour!

3 Word search

Find ten words in the box and put them in the sentences below. The words go → and ↓.

V	C	H	A	R	A	C	T	E	R	I	Z	A	T	I	O	N	P	G	L
L	C	A	P	A	R	T	H	E	I	D	Q	S	X	T	I	O	J	S	G
O	G	B	S	F	K	T	U	I	O	B	U	R	E	C	O	R	D	U	D
X	B	R	E	A	T	H	X	Q	D	M	X	G	C	E	T	Z	L	R	I
D	I	I	D	S	T	D	O	M	I	N	A	T	E	D	A	A	T	V	S
G	F	S	H	O	R	T	H	A	N	D	S	C	M	O	R	P	P	E	H
A	B	R	I	D	G	E	D	W	W	E	A	L	T	H	K	D	F	Y	W

1. I read a _____ that said that many teenagers spend too much time online.
2. Read the story and write a _____ of one of the characters.
3. Writing in _____ is a way to take notes faster.
4. _____ was a racist system in South Africa.
5. I can't watch my favourite TV show tonight, so I'm going to _____ it.
6. The smell was so nasty that I had to hold my _____.
7. India was _____ by the British until 1947.
8. Even if India has become successful in the IT industry, only a few people find _____ there.
9. This is the _____ version of a famous novel.
10. Tonight we are going to prepare an Indian _____.

Language 1

→ pages 17/18

What do you remember?

Hast du die Fotos gesehen, die Jenny gestern **online gestellt** hat?	Have you seen the photos that Jenny _____ yesterday?
Sie verbringt gerade ein Jahr in (**Spitzname für Australien**).	She is spending a year in _____ .
Gestern war sie bei einer **Grillparty** auf einer **Dachterrasse**.	Yesterday she was at a _____ (= _____) on a _____ .
Sie hatten **vielerlei exotisches** Essen.	They had _____ _____ food.
Ihre Freunde **brachten sie dazu**, **Emu**fleisch zu probieren. – **Lecker!**	Her friends _____ her try _____ meat. – _____ !
Sie hatten sogar **Krokodil**fleisch.	They even had _____ meat.
Sie war froh, dass es keine **Holzbohrerlarven** oder **grüne Ameisen** gab.	She was glad that there were no _____ or _____ .
Igitt! Ich könnte das niemals essen! – Du hast zu viele **vorgefasste Meinungen**. Probier's doch mal!	Ugh! I could never eat that! – You have too many _____ . Try it!

4 Say it in a different way

Fill in the missing word. The two sentences must have the same meaning.

1. At the party there was a lot of exotic food. → At the party there were many exotic _____ .

2. Describe the character of the hero. → Write a _____ of the hero.

3. Put the photos online on your website. → _____ the photos to your website.

4. My parents forced me to study harder.
   → My parents _____ me study harder.

5. There were so many people in the pub that you couldn't move.
   → The pub was so _____ that you couldn't move.

6. The indigenous population of Australia has a unique culture.
   → The _____ have a unique culture.

eleven 11

1 Language

→ page 17/18

What do you remember?

Australien war **früher** eine **Strafkolonie**.	Australia _____ be a _____ .
Sträflinge wurden dorthin geschickt.	_____ were sent there.
Auf dem [coat of arms] ist ein Känguru.	There is a kangaroo on the _____ .
Diese **Schiffsladung** Bananen muss heute **geliefert** werden.	This _____ of bananas must be _____ today.
Ich brauche jede **Information**, die ich über die **asiatisch-pazifische** Kultur bekommen kann.	I need every _____ about the _____ culture I can get.
Ich will **mein Auto reparieren lassen**.	I want to _____ .
In der Nähe gibt es eine Werkstatt.	There is a garage _____ .
In dieser **Version** des Films können wir einen völlig neuen **Aspekt** finden.	In this _____ of the movie, we can find a completely new _____ .
Einer meiner **Vorfahren** war ein **Krimineller**.	One of my _____ was a _____ .
Ben hatte gestern seinen **erstmaligen** Besuch auf dem deutschen **Konsulat**.	Yesterday Ben had his _____ visit to the German _____ .
Erlaube mir, dir bei diesem **Formular** zu helfen.	_____ help you with this _____ .

5 Odd word out

Find the word that doesn't fit and cross it out. Then write down why it doesn't fit in.

1. convict   ancestor   criminal   prisoner   _____
2. koala   kangaroo   elephant   platypus   _____
3. down under   Oz   Australia   G'day   _____
4. forest   tundra   rainforest   survey   _____

Writing texts 1

→ page 20

What do you remember?

Nächstes Jahr werde ich eine **Tour** quer durch Mexico machen.	Next year I'm going to go on a _____ across Mexico.	☐
Ich werde nicht vor Oktober **zurückkehren**.	I'm not going to _____ until October.	☐
point of view =	_____	☐
Was ist der **Wendepunkt** der Geschichte?	What is the _____ of the story?	☐
Ich weiß es nicht. Kannst du mir einen **Hinweis** geben?	I don't know. Can you give me a _____?	☐
Sei nicht so ein **Grübler**!	Don't be such a _____!	☐
Kontrolle durch Gleichaltrige ist eine gute Möglichkeit, eure Texte zu korrigieren.	_____ is a good way to correct your texts.	☐
Der Roman hatte einen unerwarteten **Höhepunkt**.	The novel had an unexpected _____.	☐
Hör auf, dich **prinzessinnenhaft** zu verhalten!	Stop behaving _____!	☐
Schriftsteller benutzen **Vorahnungen**, aber manchmal sind sie nur **Ablenkungsmanöver**.	Writers use _____, but sometimes the hints are just _____.	☐

6 Matching

Match the words with the right definitions.

1. characterization
2. foreshadowing
3. plot
4. setting
5. perspective
6. turning point
7. red-herring
8. climax

a) the place and time in which the story is set
b) the most exciting point of the story
c) the point in the story when the situation suddenly changes
d) a description of the qualities of the people in the story
e) a hint that leads the reader down a false path
f) hints to what might happen later on in the story
g) the action of the story
h) the point of view from which the story is told

thirteen 13

1 Wordwise

→ page 21

What do you remember?

Dieser Club **soll** der beste in London **sein**.	This club _____ the best in London.
Heute Abend gehe ich zu einem sehr **förmlichen** Abendessen.	Tonight I'm going to a very _____ dinner.
Der Präsident **gilt als** fairer Mann.	The new president _____ a fair man.

7 Peter's blog

Peter is going on a four week road trip across Australia. He is sharing his experiences in a blog. Here are two texts he has posted. Complete them with the missing words. Put them into the right form where necessary.

`exotic`   `rainforest`   `G'day`   `ozone layer`   `kangaroo`   `to destroy`
`Aussie`   `down under`   `worry-wart`   `outback`   `skin cancer`

Hi everybody out there – or, like the _____ say: "_____" :-).
Tonight I arrived in Australia and I'm dog-tired after the long flight. I'm so excited about the next four weeks _____ !! From the plane I could see the _____ and huge areas of green _____ . I'm looking forward to seeing some _____ and other _____ animals!
And here's a note for my mum: Don't be such a _____ ! :-)
I know there's a high risk of _____ , because of the _____ _____ , so I promise to wear clothes when I go to the beach. Good night everybody!

`to interest`   `used to`   `Aboriginal`   `dish`   `green ant`   `climax`   `convict`
`to make`   `barbie`   `penal colony`   `all kinds of`   `to post`   `aspect`   `crocodile`

Today some Aussies invited us over to their place. They told me that Australia _____ be a _____ . This _____ me a lot! Centuries ago, Australia was full of British _____ ! At the _____ our new friends ate _____ exotic _____ : _____ meat, for example. And they _____ us try everything! :-) I even ate _____ .
You don't believe me?! Look at the photo I have _____ ! This was the _____ of my trip – at least until now! Tomorrow I'm going to visit an _____ reservation to get to know a different _____ of Australian culture. See you!

Check-out 1

8 A crossword

Complete the crossword puzzle with the missing words in the sentences.

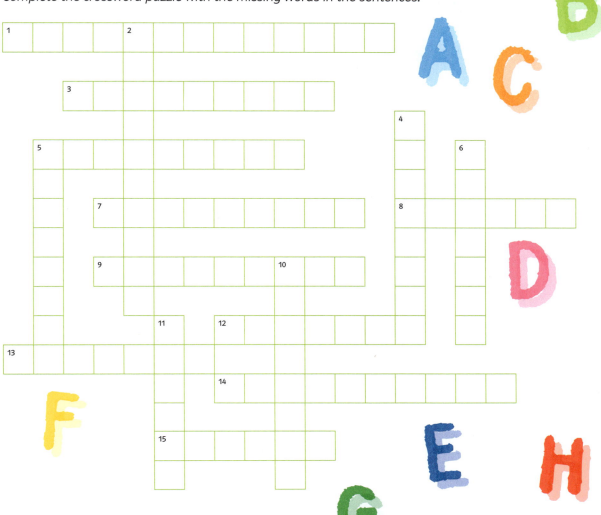

ACROSS	DOWN
1. The writer used a lot of … to create expectations in the reader. 3. After a war there are often many … families. 5. The company is looking for someone who is able to write in … 7. The … will help you if you get into trouble in a foreign country, for example if you lose your passport. 8. Skin … is a problem in Australia. 9. The political system of Germany is … 12. I can speak three … languages: French, Spanish and Italian. 13. The story was … for children. 14. The Aborigines are the … population of Australia. 15. Jimmy likes Maths and working with money, so he decided to become a …	2. After World War II America became a … 4. The president soon realized that the … was lost. 5. The workers are waiting for a … of steel. 6. The Queen is the British … 10. Only the … version of the film is shown in the cinema. 11. Let's go to the small shop … I must buy some food.

2 Check-in

Unit 2 What next?

→ pages 28/29

What do you remember?

Es ist nicht einfach einen **Beruf** zu wählen.	It's not easy to choose a _____.
In Großbritannien kann man nach dem **allg. Abschluss der weiterführenden Schulen** weiter **lernen**.	After the _____ (= _____) you can continue to _____.
Ich weiß nicht, ob ich das **britische Abitur** schreiben soll.	I don't know if I should take _____.
Ich mag keine **Prüfungen**.	I don't like _____.
Ich würde ein **Praktikum** als vorziehen.	I would prefer _____ as a _____.
Ich würde gerne **Sozialarbeit** machen, bevor ich mit der **Hochschulbildung** weitermache.	I'd like to do _____ before I go on to _____.
Peter will **Architekt** werden.	Peter wants to become an _____.
Linda will ins Ausland gehen, um **Fremdsprachen** zu lernen.	Linda wants to go abroad to study _____.

1 Jumbled words

Put the letters into the right order to complete the sentences.

Jerry: Hi Gina, have you already decided what to do after your _____ **ECSG** exams?

Gina: I think I will continue school for two more years and take my _____ **ELVE-ALS**. After that I could go on to _____ **IHRHEG TODUNICEA** and maybe become an _____ **HECTICRAT**. What about you?

Jerry: Well I think I'm going to choose a _____ **ERREAC** right after the _____ **ASMEX**. I don't want to _____ **DYSUT** anymore. I like _____ **CASLIO KORW** and I'm thinking of becoming a _____ **RESUN**.

16 sixteen

Check-in 2

→ pages 28/29

What do you remember?

Ich **schrieb** gestern **eine** schwierige **Prüfung**.	I _____ a difficult _____ yesterday.	☐
Eine Laufbahn als Polizist würde nicht **zu mir passen**.	A career as a policeman wouldn't _____.	☐
Ich will keine **Leichen** sehen!	I don't want to see _____!	☐
Mein Bruder hat die **Chance** bekommen, **Musiker** zu werden.	My brother has got the _____ to become a _____.	☐
Er **erreicht** immer, was er will, denn er ist sehr **konkurrenzfähig**.	He always _____ what he wants because he's very _____.	☐
Unser **Anwalt** hat uns einen schlechten Rat gegeben.	Our _____ has given us bad advice.	☐
Er ist nicht sehr **vertrauenswürdig**.	He isn't very _____.	☐
Ich muss den **Fragebogen** ausfüllen.	I must complete the _____.	☐

2 Verbs and their friends

Match the verbs with the right words or expressions.

A-levels   Maths   a nurse   foreign languages   wealth   an exam   a lawyer   the age of 18   an architect   famous   Science   GCSEs

to take	to study	to reach	to become

3 Spot the mistakes

Find two mistakes in each sentence and write down the correct version of the sentence on the line.

1. Let's complete the questionaire for the survey on carer wishes.

   _____

2. After the CGSEs Sue went on to lower education.

   _____

seventeen **17**

2 Check-in

→ pages 28/29

What do you remember?

Was denkst du über die **Klischees** über Männer und Frauen?	What do you think about the _____ about men and women?
Ich muss zur **Bank** gehen.	I have to go to the _____.
Ben mag **praktische** Arbeit.	Ben likes _____ work.
Er interessiert sich für den **Bau**.	He is interested in _____.
Der **Personalchef** war nicht sehr **taktvoll**.	The _____ was not very _____.
Unser **Eisenbahnnetz** ist ziemlich gut entwickelt.	Our _____ is quite well-developed.
Der Zug kommt wegen **technischer** Probleme zu spät.	The train is late because of _____ problems.

4 Synonyms

Replace the marked word with a word with the same or a similar meaning.

1. I'm not sure which **job** (→ _____) to choose.

2. The **test** (→ _____) was very easy for me.

3. The competition was a great **chance** (→ _____) to change my life.

5 Word search

Find ten words in the box. The words go → and ↓.

P	V	F	S	T	E	R	E	O	T	Y	P	E	W	P
R	R	U	T	R	E	A	E	T	Z	U	C	A	B	M
A	A	Q	U	E	S	T	I	O	N	N	A	I	R	E
C	A	L	D	L	Y	A	A	S	R	U	R	I	V	A
T	T	M	Y	I	R	E	N	U	R	S	E	Y	H	K
I	U	B	V	A	A	R	C	H	I	T	E	C	T	U
C	O	O	U	B	A	N	K	C	G	O	R	V	N	T
A	P	U	O	L	I	O	S	R	U	O	N	O	O	R
L	K	T	T	E	C	H	N	I	C	A	L	O	P	B

18 eighteen

Language 1 2

→ pages 30–32

What do you remember?

Sarah möchte nach der Schule auf die **Universität** gehen.	Sarah would like to go to _____ after school.
Sie ist ein **kluger Kopf**.	She's a _____ .
Sie wird mit einem **Berater** über das **Image** verschiedener Universitäten sprechen.	She is going to talk to an _____ about the _____ of different universities.
Mein **Gehalt** ist nicht sehr hoch, aber ich werde mich **hocharbeiten**.	My _____ isn't very high at the moment, but I'm going to _____ .
Der **Abgabetermin** ist nächsten Donnerstag.	The _____ is next Thursday.
Wenn Sie Fragen haben, wenden Sie sich bitte an unsere **Beratungsstelle**.	If you have any questions, please contact our _____ .

6 Say it in a different way

Fill in the missing word. The two sentences must have the same meaning.

1. In my job, I don't earn much money. → The _____ for my job is very low.

2. It wouldn't be good for Ben to become a doctor, because he can't stand seeing blood.
   → A career as a doctor wouldn't _____ Ben, because he can't stand seeing blood.

3. The article must be written by Monday. → The _____ for the article is Monday.

4. This university is supposed to be good. → This university has a good _____ .

7 What about you?

Write down what you would like to do after you've finished school. (If you don't know yet, you can make something up.) Use at least six of the following words.

A-levels · foreign language · to suit sth · social work · to reach · university · pay · to be involved (in) · to study · higher education · to work one's way up · exam · competitive · practical · opportunity

_____
_____
_____
_____

2 Language 1

→ pages 30–32

What do you remember?

Schau, da ist ein **Informationsblatt** über eine Party für die Altersgruppe ab 16 **aufwärts**.	Look, there's a _____ about a party for the 16 _____ (_____) age group.
Der Filmstar will einen neuen **Friseur einstellen**.	The movie star wants to _____ a new _____ .
Ben isst **hauptsächlich** Gemüse.	Ben _____ eats vegetables.
Ich kann nicht ausgehen, weil ich einen **Abgabetermin einhalten** muss.	I can't go out because I have to _____ .
Du wirst **mich** nicht **davon abbringen**, dieses Computerspiel zu kaufen.	You aren't going to _____ buying this computer game.
Diese Jeans hat eine gute **Qualität**.	The _____ of these jeans is good.
In der **Multimedia**welt gibt es eine hohe **Konkurrenz**.	In the _____ world there's lots of _____ .
to go up =	_____

8 Word formation

Find a word from the same word family.

1. to pay → (noun) _____
2. to practice → (adjective) _____
3. music → (noun) _____
4. main → (adverb) _____
5. competition → (adjective) _____
6. bank → (noun) _____
7. question → (noun) _____
8. law → (noun) _____

9 Mixed bag

Put in the missing words.

1 I know that the skirt is very expensive, but I really want to have it.

   You won't _____ buying it.

2 I have many good _____ . I'm tactful and reliable, for example.

3 Ronny hasn't got any problems at school. He's a real _____ .

Writing texts 2

→ page 33

What do you remember?

Mein **Geburtsdatum** ist der 15. Dezember 1996.	My _____ is 15 December, 1996.
Ich habe gute technische **Kenntnisse**.	I've got a good technical _____ .
In den Ferien möchte Jane als **Freiwillige** arbeiten.	In the holidays, Jane would like to work as a _____ .
Architektur passt nicht zu mir.	_____ doesn't suit me.
Bis jetzt habe ich zehn **Bewerbungsschreiben** geschrieben.	So far I have written ten _____ .
Ich **lege** meinen **Lebenslauf** und ein **Referenzschreiben** bei.	I _____ my _____ (= _____) and a _____ .
Dies ist eine **Bewerbung** um ein **Praktikum**.	This is an _____ for a _____ .
Die Internetseite **steht** im Moment nicht **zur Verfügung**.	The website is not _____ at the moment.
Garry möchte sich **um** den Job **bewerben**.	Garry wants to _____ the job.
Ich muss den Brief **ausdrucken** und meine **Unterschrift** hinzufügen.	I must _____ the letter and add my _____ .
Mit freundlichen Grüßen, Kathy Brown	_____ , Kathy Brown.
Anlage: Lebenslauf	_____ CV

10 Style

A letter of application must be written in a formal style. Rewrite the following sentences.

My friend John told me about the job as a hairdresser and I'm writing because I want to do it. I always cut my mum's hair, so I think I'd do a good job. I like chatting with people, so I think I could have a lot of fun during work …

_____
_____
_____
_____

2 Language 2

→ pages 34/35

What do you remember?

Sarah spricht vier Fremdsprachen **fließend**.	Sarah is _____ in four foreign languages.
Der **Meteorologe sagte** gutes Wetter **voraus**.	The _____ _____ good weather.
Ich sah es heute Abend in der **Wettervorhersage**.	I saw it on the _____ tonight.
Ich bin nicht sicher, ob ich in die richtige **Richtung** gehe.	I'm not sure if I'm going in the right _____.
Ich habe heute einen **Termin** mit Herrn Lee.	I've got an _____ with Mr Lee today.
Meteorologie interessiert mich nicht sehr.	_____ doesn't interest me much.
Das **Wartezimmer** beim Zahnarzt war überfüllt.	The _____ at the dentist's was crowded.

11 Career crossword

Write down the clues for the words in the crossword puzzle.

Crossword:
1 across: MUSICIAN
Down: METEOROLOGIST
2 down: HAIRDRESSER
3 across: BANKER
4 down: NURSE
5 across: LAWYER
6 across: TEACHER

ACROSS
1. _____
3. _____
5. _____
6. _____

DOWN
1. _____
2. _____
4. _____

22 twenty-two

Language 2

→ pages 34/35

What do you remember?

Jenny **schwebt** immer **über den Dingen**.	Jenny always _____.
Wirst schon sehen, unsere Mannschaft wird gewinnen!	_____, our team is going to win!
Wir **haben uns** für einen neuen Spieler **entschieden**.	We've _____ a new player.
Sein Name ist Stefano Cami… **Dingsda**.	His name is Stefano Cami… _____.
Camilleri, **Dummkopf**. Er ist Italiener.	Camilleri, _____. He's Italian.
Das Abendessen ist **serviert**!	Dinner is _____!
Alles wird **klappen**!	Everything is going to _____!
Die Konkurrenz ist **groß**, deswegen muss ich wirklich gut sein.	The competition is _____, so I have to be really good.
sehen, *hören* und *fühlen* sind **Verben der Wahrnehmung**.	*see*, *hear* and *feel* are _____.

12 Find the missing word

1. concert • musician weather forecast • _____	3. to push • to pull to fall • _____	5. lawyer • career south • _____
2. architect • architecture meteorologist • _____	4. manager • assistant doctor • _____	6. career • to work university • _____

13 Verbs

Complete the grid adding four verbs to each category.

phrasal verbs	verbs of perception	irregular verbs
to turn off	to look	to shake

twenty-three 23

2 Talkwise

→ page 37

What do you remember?

Sally **hatte** gestern **ein Vorstellungsgespräch**.	Sally _____ yesterday.
Sie denkt, sie **hat einen schlechten Eindruck gemacht**.	She thinks she _____ .
Sie denkt, sie hat nicht genug auf ihre **Körpersprache** geachtet.	She thinks she didn't pay enough attention to her _____ .
Der **Leiter des Vorstellungsgespräches** war sehr nett.	The _____ was very nice.
Er hatte einen guten **Eindruck** von der **Bewerberin**.	He had a good _____ of the _____ .
Sally ist **geeignet** für die Stelle.	Sally is _____ for the job.
Sie wurde vom **Arbeitgeber** angenommen.	She was accepted by the _____ .

14 Correct the sentences

Change one word in every sentence to make it right.

1. In an interview it is very important to make a bad impression. _____
2. The employer is the one who wants to get the job. _____
3. At the end of a letter you add your website. _____
4. When you go to the doctor's you often have to sit in the living room for a while. _____
5. Being able to meet friends is very important when you are a journalist. _____

15 Bits and pieces

Form words from the syllables.

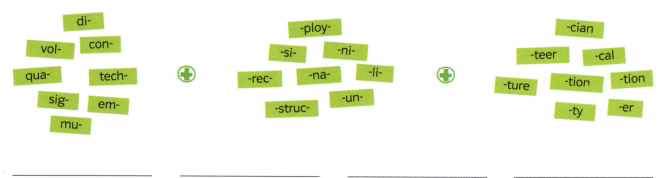

_____   _____   _____   _____

_____   _____   _____   _____

Text 2

→ pages 38–40

What do you remember?

Zeitung	Many people look for a job in the _____.
Prüfung bestehen	After you _____ your final _____ at school, there are many different possibilities.
Gärtner • Politiker	Should you become a _____, a teacher, a nurse, a _____, a musician or a _____?
halbtags	Would it be possible to work only _____?
beeinflusst sein von	It's important not to _____ too much by what your friends do. Try to find out what you like and what suits you.
Kaum zu glauben! • Kindheit	_____! It can even be helpful to think of what you wanted to become in your _____.
sich ausdenken	Career plans you _____ back then can already show you something about yourself and your qualities.

16 A job interview

Barry is being interviewed for a job as a nurse. Write down his answers.

Interviewer: Tell me something about yourself.

Barry sagt, dass er nach den GCSEs soziale Arbeit geleistet und ein Praktikum in einem Krankenhaus gemacht hat.

Barry: _____

_____

Interviewer: Why have you chosen a career as a nurse?

Barry antwortet, dass Medizin ihn schon immer interessiert hat und er praktische Arbeit mag.

Barry: _____

Interviewer: Please tell me about your positive qualities.

Barry sagt, dass er denkt, er sei zuverlässig und dass er gut mit Menschen umgehen kann.

Barry: _____

Interviewer: Well, Barry, that all sounds very good. We'll let you know when we've made a decision.

twenty-five 25

2 Text

→ pages 38–40

What do you remember?

herumdrehen • gehen	Jimmy and his family were living in an old bus, but one day, when his dad _____ the wheel, it said: "I _____!"
auf den Kopf gestellt	It went off the road and stopped _____.
• schnappen	After that they were living in a _____, but one day it was _____ by a tornado.
mitten • hin und her werfen	Then they were living on a boat but one day _____ the night they were _____ by a storm.
sich am Riemen reißen	Because they didn't have enough to live off, the kids told their dad to _____.
Wohnwagen	From then on they were living in a _____.

17 How does the text say it?

Without looking at the text in your pupil's book again, rewrite the sentences using the words from the story.

1. […] and finally stops with its wheels in the air.
   → "[…] and finally stops _____ on its roof."

2. […] one day the poor old tent is blown away by a tornado […].
   → "[…] one day the poor old tent _____ by a tornado […]."

3. But their unusual childhood has had an influence on them all.
   → "But every one of them is _____ by their unusual childhood […]."

4. […] I'm sure that's what story-telling is about, inventing it while you are telling the story.
   → "[…] I'm sure that's what story-telling is about, _____ as you go along."

18 Jumbled words

Put the letters into the right order.

1. NETT _____
2. DULEBIR _____
3. LIEARTR _____
4. HODOCDILH _____
5. NILTIOPIAC _____
6. GENDERAR _____

Text 2

→ pages 38–40

What do you remember?

afrikanisch • heilen • Krankheiten •	Jimmy became a doctor and went to the _____ country Congo where he _____ _____ with only very few _____ .
Kampagne • betteln um • Medizin • leiden	He travelled to America, doing a _____ for Africa, _____ _____ and money for the people who _____ there.
Stöckchen	Some of them had arms and legs like _____ .
zusammenarbeitend	He thought that with _____ work we could help them.
Es ist an euch •	"_____", he said to the people and they all opened their _____ .
Gabe	Jimmy had a special _____ .

19 Words and pictures

Write down what you can see in the pictures.

1 _____ 2 _____ 3 _____ 4 _____

20 Mixed bag

Fill in the right words.

1. I've got a _____ job at the moment. I work only in the mornings.

2. This story Ben told me yesterday can't be true! I'm sure he _____ it _____ !

3. Why are you calling me _____ the night?

4. Carol doesn't want to drive. She _____ still _____ by the car accident last month.

5. Oh dear, I can't find my _____ ! There were more than $ 200 in it.

twenty-seven 27

2 Wordwise

→ page 41

What do you remember?

Mit **Nachsilben** kann man neue Wörter formen.	With _____ you can form new words.	☐
Morgen **wird** es **wahrscheinlich** regnen.	It _____ rain tomorrow.	☐
Stell das Glas nicht dorthin! Es **wird sicher** herunterfallen.	Don't put the glass there! It _____ fall down.	☐

21 Word families

Find two words that belong to the same word family.

1. musician _____
2. unhappy _____
3. employment _____
4. training _____

22 Sally's first interview

For the first time Sally is being interviewed for a job. Being very nervous she makes some mistakes. Say what she should do better next time.

1. She cannot find the place, so she is 15 minutes late.

   _____

   _____

2. When the door is opened she goes in and takes a seat. Then she says 'hello' to the interviewer.

   _____

   _____

3. She is very tired because she went out with her friends the night before, so she answers several questions only with 'yes' and 'no'.

   _____

   _____

4. When she is asked if she has got any questions, she only wants to know how much she would be paid.

   _____

   _____

28 twenty-eight

Check-out 2

→ pages 42/43

What do you remember?

Da ist eine interessante **Anzeige** in der Zeitung.	There's an interesting _____ in the newspaper.	☐
Meine **Arbeitsstätte** ist in einem hohen Gebäude.	My _____ is in a high building.	☐
Schreibe einen **Adverbialsatz** auf.	Write down an _____ .	☐

23 Word parts

Put the word parts together to complete the sentences.

cam · ler · paign · disea · able · volun · ment · eer · employ · appli · musi · child · pre · trai · ent · car · suit · appli · appoint · er · law · cian · cant · ses · eign · hood · sion · yer · dicts · cation · impres · teer · flu · for

1. The weather forecast _____ a big storm.
2. Although I grew up without a father, my _____ was very happy.
3. The _____ made a very good _____ in the interview.
4. I have to send a letter of _____ to my new _____ .
5. In some countries there are many _____ and not enough drugs.
6. I have an _____ with my _____ at 10 o'clock.
7. Last year I worked as a _____ helping poor children in Mexico.
8. The president's _____ was the most expensive one of this year's elections.
9. Danny is _____ in three _____ languages.
10. I'm not sure which _____ is _____ for me.
11. Jamie loves playing the guitar. He'd like to become a _____ .
12. Some families are very poor and have to live in a _____ .

twenty-nine 29

Revision Unit 1 + 2

1 Australia

Make a word web about Australia.

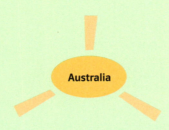

2 Your interview

You are being interviewed for a job as a _____ (your choice). Answer the interviewer's questions.

Interviewer: Tell me something about yourself.

You: _____
_____
_____

Interviewer: Why would you like to work for our company?

You: _____
_____

Interviewer: Why do you think that you are suitable for this kind of work?

You: _____
_____

Interviewer: What are your negative qualities?

You: _____
_____

Interviewer: Do you have any questions?

You: _____
_____

Unit 3   Media-mad

→ pages 50–53

What do you remember?

bedecken	They have _____ their classroom with posters.
bequem	I love my bed. It's really _____ .
beweisen	Can you _____ that this poem was all your own work?
Nur zu!	"Can I have some more chips please?" – "_____!"
direkt	If you want Anna's help, speak to her _____ .
	Those lions have been _____ all night. They must be hungry!
sich wohl fühlen	I don't _____ at a party if I don't know anyone.

1 Jumbled words

Put the letters in the correct order to complete the sentences.

1. I can _____ that I am fourteen. Here's my ID card. **EPVOR**
2. I feel very _____ when I am with my family and friends. **TOMEBALCROF**
3. If you want to play more tennis, speak _____ to your sports teacher. **RYDTICEL**
4. It's raining! _____ the food quickly. We'll finish the picnic later. **VROCE**
5. "Can I take your photo?" – "_____ !" **OGHADAE**
6. Just listen to that lion _____ . It must be hungry. **GRAROIN**

2 One letter – different sounds

How do we pronounce the letter o in these words? Write the words in the correct box.

cover   prove   lose   comfortable   money   move   two   love

[ʌ]	[uː]

3 Text A + B

→ pages 50–53

What do you remember?

Macht	Famous people can have a lot of _____ over young people.
Tonspur	Most songs have a lot of different _____.
	My parents let me watch _____ for an hour every evening.
medienverrückt	Tom's _____. He's always on the Internet or watching TV.

3 Media crossword

Read the clues and complete the crossword.

ACROSS
1. The media have the … to change our ideas.
3. These tell us about new products.
4. My favourite television … is *Sports Today*.
6. Most people watch this after school or work.
7. Someone who loves the media is …
8. Songs often have different … for instruments and voices.

DOWN
2. In the past, people listened to the radio for this.
5. We can go to the cinema to see these.

Skills + Language 3

→ pages 54–56

What do you remember?

Ich habe wirklich guten **Tratsch** über Amy gehört!	I've heard some really good _____ about Amy.
Online-Netzwerke sind eine gute Möglichkeit, mit all deinen Freunden zu reden.	_____ are a great way to talk to all your friends.
Das Aussehen einer Person ist für mich **ohne Bedeutung**.	A person's looks are _____ to me.
Ich will nicht **heiraten**, bevor ich 25 bin.	I don't want to _____ until I am twenty-five.
Man sollte immer höflich **argumentieren**, auch wenn man eine starke Meinung zu einem Thema hat.	You should always _____ politely, even if you have a strong opinion on a topic.
Eva hat mir erzählt, dass du mit Kevin **zusammen bist**. Er ist sehr nett!	Eva told me you _____ Kevin. He's really nice!
Ich **bin unfähig** zu lernen, wenn es zu laut ist.	I _____ study when there's too much noise.
Man sollte sein Handy **keinesfalls** im Unterricht benutzen.	_____ should you use your mobile phone in class.
	Your _____ controls every movement of your body.
Ich kann die Nachrichten im **Videotext** nachsehen.	I can check _____ for the news.
Du bist so clever! Was für eine **Intelligenz** du besitzt!	You're so clever! What _____ you have!
Heutzutage haben die meisten ein Smartphone.	_____, most people have a smartphone.
Ich schreibe **als Reaktion auf** Ihre E-Mail vom 6. Mai.	I am writing _____ your e-mail of 6th May.

4 Odd one out

Underline the word or phrase that doesn't fit in.

1. gossip • study • argue • chat
2. see someone • fall in love • split up • get married
3. No way! • Sorry, I can't. • I'm unable to right now. • Of course!
4. in the past • in the present • these days • in the 21st century

3 Skills + Language

→ pages 54–56

What do you remember?

Ihr **gesprochenes** Englisch ist exzellent, aber ihr **geschriebenes** Englisch ist weniger gut.	Her _____ English is excellent, but her _____ English is not as good.
Kannst du das erste Kapitel des Buchs **zusammenfassen**?	Can you _____ the first chapter of the book?
Was ist dein **Standpunkt** zum Problem des Regenwalds?	What's your _____ on the problem of the rainforest?
Filtere die Fakten, um die wichtigsten zu erhalten.	_____ the facts to get the most important ones.
Ich bin sehr gut darin, **mehrere Dinge gleichzeitig zu tun**.	I'm really good at _____ !
Gesundheit und Fitness sind wichtige **Themen**.	Health and fitness are very important _____ .
Musik hat einen positiven **Effekt** auf viele Menschen.	Music has a positive _____ on many people.
Ich kann das Auto vor uns wegen des Regens **kaum** sehen.	I can _____ see the car in front because of the rain.
Dein Haar ist sehr glänzend. Welches **Shampoo** benutzt du?	Your hair's really shiny – what _____ do you use?
Welche **Quelle** hast du für die Informationen benutzt?	Which _____ did you use for the information?

5 Mixed bag: The presentation

A teacher is giving her pupils instructions about giving a presentation. Fill the gaps with these words.

written   view   source   filter   spoken   effect   issue   summarize

"OK, so first you need to think of an _____ that your classmates will find interesting. Look at lots of websites and read as much as you can. Make a lot of notes, then _____ the information so you have only the most useful ideas to work with. _____ the main points, then decide which parts of your presentation will be _____ and which parts will be _____ . You'll need to give the _____ of your information (which websites did you use?) and find some fun pictures too, if you want to have a big _____ on your audience. Make sure you give your own _____ clearly, and be ready to answer questions. Off you go – good luck!"

34 thirty-four

Writing texts 3

→ page 58

What do you remember?

( ) Dies nennt man **Klammern**.	( ) These are called _____ .
Ich habe für meinen Artikel **Normalschrift** verwendet.	I used _____ for my article.
*Diese Wörter sind in **Kursivschrift***.	*These words are in _____ .*
Wir benutzen eine **Totale**, damit wir das Haus sehen können.	We'll use a _____ so we can see the house.
Dann können wir eine **Nahaufnahme** des Küchenfensters machen.	Then we can do a _____ of the kitchen window.
Lasst uns für die Liebesszene **Dämmerlicht** verwenden.	Let's use _____ for the love scene.
Vielleicht könnte das Paar ein **romantisches** Essen bei Kerzenschein haben.	Maybe the couple could have a _____ meal by candle light.
Jetzt **zoomen** wir **heran**, um sein Gesicht deutlich zu sehen.	Now, we _____ so that we can see his face clearly.
Das ist eine wunderschöne **Einstellung** der Berge.	That's a beautiful _____ of the mountains.
Hört auf die **Anweisungen**, damit ihr wisst, was zu tun ist.	Listen to the _____ so you know what to do.
Versuche eine **Halbnahe**, nicht zu nah und nicht zu weit.	Try a _____ , not too close and not too wide.

6 Word fields

Write the words from the boxes under the right heading.

zoom-in   brackets   medium shot   catch phrase   wide shot
normal type   soft lighting   italics   close-up   directions

Camera work	Script writing
_____	_____
_____	_____
_____	_____
_____	_____
_____	_____

thirty-five **35**

3 Writing texts

→ page 58

What do you remember?

Warum **zuckst** du **mit den Schultern**? Weißt du die Antwort nicht?	Why are you _____? Don't you know the answer?
Was **lutschst** du da? – Dein letztes Zitronenbonbon!	What are you _____? – Your last lemon sweet!
Mary **ist** wirklich **sauer auf** Joey. Er hat ihre CD verloren.	Mary's really _____ Joey. He's lost her CD.
Komm schon, **triff eine Wahl**! Eis oder Kuchen?	Come on, _____! Ice-cream or cake?
Warum **hast du dich von mir abgewendet**, als ich gewunken habe?	Why did you _____ when I waved at you?
Jede gute Werbung hat einen **Slogan**, den sich jeder merken kann.	Every good ad has a _____ that we all remember.
Wir hatten **statt** eines normalen Mittagessens ein Picknick.	We had a picnic _____ a normal lunch.
Tom spricht sehr deutlich – ich finde, er sollte den **Hintergrundkommentar** sprechen.	Tom speaks very clearly – I think he should do the _____ .
Rob **ist verrückt nach** Fußball. Er liebt ihn!	Rob's _____ football. He loves it!

7 Spot the mistake

Underline the wrong preposition in each sentence and correct it.

1. My brother is mad of me because I ate the last piece of cake. _____
2. The film was so sad – Mel was at tears. _____
3. If you don't know the words to the song, just make them off. _____
4. Luke turned away to his sister when she started shouting at him. _____
5. Why don't you go outside instead in watching TV all day? _____
6. Can you help me look out my mobile? I can't find it anywhere. _____
7. I don't care of you any more – do what you want. _____
8. Lisa's mad on dancing – she dances wherever she can. _____

Wordwise 3

→ page 59

What do you remember?

Wegen des schlechten Wetters blieben wir am Sonntag zu Hause.	We stayed at home on Sunday _____ the bad weather.
Die Polizei kennt die **Ursache** für den Unfall nicht.	The police don't know the _____ of the accident.
Die Männer **fesselten** den Verkäufer und stahlen das ganze Geld.	The men _____ the shop assistant and stole all the money.
Du hast deine Hausaufgaben nicht fertig, **deshalb** kannst du nicht fernsehen!	You haven't finished your homework, _____ you can't watch television!
Ich ging um neun ins Bett, **weil** ich sehr müde war.	I went to bed at nine _____ I was really tired.
Die **örtlichen** Läden in meiner Gegend sind wirklich langweilig.	The _____ shops in my area are really boring.
Ivy half Jim bei seinen Hausaufgaben, **da** sie gut in Mathe ist.	Ivy helped Jim with his homework _____ she's good at Maths.
	There is always someone who _____ outside the café in town.

8 Sentence matching

Match the beginnings and endings of these sentences.

1. The cause of my headache
2. I got a headache because
3. Can you help me as
4. Can you help me so
5. The car broke down because
6. The car broke down, therefore
7. She missed the party because of
8. She missed the party because

- we were late.
- she was ill.
- was too much sun.
- the sun was too hot.
- her exam.
- I can finish this quickly?
- it was so old.
- you're so good at Maths?

3 Check-out

→ page 60

What do you remember?

Emma Goodman **tritt** fast jeden Tag im Fernsehen **auf**.	Emma Goodman _____ on TV nearly every day.	☐
In zwei Wochen werde ich mit meiner Familie im Urlaub sein. Ich kann es gar nicht erwarten!	Two weeks _____, I'll be on holiday with my family. I can't wait!	☐
Guten Abend, liebe **Zuschauer**. Willkommen zur Sendung!	Good evening, _____. Welcome to the show!	☐

9 Word search: The media

There are 10 media words hidden in this word search. The words go ↓, ↑, ← and →. Find them and write them down on the lines.

R	O	M	T	N	E	M	N	I	A	T	R	E	T	N	E	P	B	L	M	N
E	N	X	E	S	M	Y	O	W	U	G	L	U	C	X	Q	H	Z	Y	R	O
P	K	I	L	D	C	A	M	E	R	A	S	H	O	T	U	N	O	A	Y	I
A	D	V	E	R	T	I	S	E	M	E	N	T	I	V	A	W	O	X	Z	T
P	P	G	T	U	D	S	P	O	H	Y	B	M	J	W	X	R	M	O	N	C
S	X	R	E	V	O	E	C	I	O	V	Y	L	I	G	H	T	I	N	G	E
W	Y	D	X	P	D	I	H	P	R	C	C	X	U	L	A	T	N	Q	P	R
E	A	J	T	E	L	E	V	I	S	I	O	N	B	O	Z	C	F	P	G	I
N	P	L	F	J	G	F	I	D	O	F	U	F	X	E	Q	D	X	I	M	D

_____

_____

_____

10 Definitions

Which words are described? Write them down.

1. Something you take with a camera: _____

2. A person who watches a television programme: _____

3. An important topic that people talk about: _____

4. The written version of a movie: _____

5. The title of a newspaper article: _____

Unit 4 Human rights

→ pages 68/69

What do you remember?

Menschenrechte und **Toleranz** sind wichtige Themen.	_____ and _____ are important topics.
Eine **kürzlich** erschienene Studie **sagt aus**, dass nur wenige Länder **die Voraussetzungen** für eine **demokratische** Gesellschaft **erfüllen**.	A _____ study _____ that only a few countries _____ as a _____ society.
Gleichgeschlechtliche Beziehungen werden immer noch nicht in allen Ländern akzeptiert.	_____ _____ still aren't accepted in every country.
Dies sind Beziehungen zwischen **homosexuellen** Männern oder **lesbischen** Frauen.	These are relationships between _____ men or _____ women.
Mitglieder des **Parlaments**, die eine **Machtposition** haben, sollten mit gutem Beispiel vorangehen.	Members of _____, who are in a _____, should set a good example.

1 Just for fun: Songs about human rights

Read the complete song lyrics on the Internet or find out more about the bands who wrote the human rights songs.

As soon as you're born they make you feel small
By giving you no time instead of it all
Till the pain is so big you feel nothing at all
(Green Day, "Working Class Hero")

Get up, stand up: stand up for your rights!
Get up, stand up: don't give up the fight!
(Bob Marley and the Wailers, "Get Up, Stand Up")

Why are these women here dancing on their own?
Why is there this sadness in their eyes?
Why are the soldiers here
Their faces fixed like stone?
(Sting, "They dance alone")

4 Check-in

→ pages 68/69

What do you remember?

Leider haben die Menschen nicht auf der ganzen Welt die gleichen **Rechte**.	Unfortunately, people do not have the same _____ all over the world.
Die Art, wie einige Menschen behandelt werden, ist nicht **menschlich**.	The way some people are treated isn't _____.
In manchen Ländern gibt es **autoritäre Regimes**.	In some countries there are _____ _____.
Die Menschen dort besitzen keine **Redefreiheit** oder **Religions**freiheit. Noch haben sie das Recht zu **protestieren**.	The people there don't have _____ or freedom of _____. They do not have the right to _____ either.
Diese Menschen sind leider nicht **gleich**.	Sadly, these people are not _____.
Sie haben keine **Chancengleichheit** so wie die Menschen in **Demokratien**.	They do not have _____ as people in _____ do.
Dies bedeutet, dass die **Würde** des Menschen in autoritären Gesellschaften nicht wichtig ist.	This means that human _____ is not important in authoritarian societies.

2 Word stress

Which words have the same stress? Put the words into the right boxes. Then practice saying them.

religion   invention   position   especially   protest   apologize
parliament   equal   recent   democracy   dignity   commercial
industrial   human   tolerance   lesbian

• •	• • •	• • •	• • • •

40 forty

Check-in 4

→ pages 68/69

What do you remember?

Rassengleichheit bedeutet, dass Schwarze und Weiße gleich behandelt werden.	_____ means that blacks and whites are treated the same.
Martin Luther King sprach in seiner berühmten Rede über **Brüderlichkeit**.	Martin Luther King spoke about _____ in his famous speech.
Indien und China sind **Entwicklungsländer**.	India and China are part of the _____ .
Ein großer **Anteil** der Politiker sind **Männer**.	A large _____ of politicians are _____ .
Nicht viele Frauen haben hohe **Positionen** in Unternehmen.	Not many women have high _____ in companies.
Der Tag der **Arbeit** ist am 1. März.	_____ day is on the 1st March.
Die ersten Gesetze gegen **Kinderarbeit** wurden zu Beginn des 19. Jahrhunderts erlassen.	The first laws against _____ were passed at the beginning of the 19th century.
Ich muss meine Arbeit wiederholen. Sie ist nicht **zufriedenstellend**.	I have to redo my work. It isn't _____ .

3 Matching

Match the words with the right definitions.

1. parliament
2. gay
3. satisfactory
4. male
5. religion
6. child labour
7. developing world
8. freedom of speech
9. racial equality
10. democracy

a) if something is good enough
b) not a woman or girl
c) believing in (a) god(s)
d) when people under the age of 16 work
e) when black and white people are treated the same
f) when people have the right to say what they want
g) the political system in Germany
h) countries with a low standard of living
i) homosexual
j) a group of people who make or change laws

4 Check-in

→ pages 68/69

What do you remember?

Das **Geschlecht** einer Person gibt an, ob sie ein Mann oder eine Frau ist.	The _____ of a person tells you if he or she is a man or a woman.
Es ist wichtig, die Unterschiede zwischen Menschen zu **tolerieren**.	It's important to _____ differences between people.
Es gab einen **Protest** gegen den Irakkrieg.	There was a _____ against the Iraq war.
Frauen **stellen** weniger als 4 % der Politiker **dar**.	Women _____ less than 4 % of politicians.
Er hat den Job auf der **Grundlage** seiner Hautfarbe nicht bekommen.	He didn't get the job on the _____ of his skin colour.
Manche Menschen verstehen den wahren **Geist** der Brüderlichkeit nicht.	Some people don't understand the true _____ of brotherhood.
Die Vereinten Nationen haben eine Liste der **am wenigsten** entwickelten Länder erstellt.	The UN have made a list of the _____ developed countries.
Frauen **gelten** oft **als** weniger konkurrenzfähig als Männer.	Women are often _____ less competitive than men.
Diskriminierung ist ein **ständiges** Problem.	Discrimination is a _____ problem.

4 A quiz

Complete the questions with the missing words from the boxes. Can you guess the right answers? Draw lines to the answers on the right.

gay   regime   developing   democracy   parliament

1. Which European country has the highest proportion of women in _____ ?

2. Which countries are under a _____ today?

3. Is there _____ marriage in England?

4. Where does the idea of _____ come from?

5. Which countries are in the _____ world?

Sweden

Iran, North Korea and Myanmar

Yes, it was one of the first countries in the world to allow same-sex relationships.

China, India and Brazil

Greece

42 forty-two

Language 1 | 4

→ pages 70-72

What do you remember?

Die Geschichte der **Sklaverei** reicht weit zurück.	The history of _____ goes back a long time.	☐
Im **Mittelalter** war es für reiche Leute üblich, **Sklaven** zu haben.	In the _____, it used to be common for rich people to have _____.	☐
In der **Antike** wurden die **Pyramiden** von ihnen gebaut.	In _____ times, the _____ were built by them.	☐
Reiche Menschen wurden noch reicher, **indem** sie andere **gewaltsam** dazu brachten, für sie zu arbeiten.	Rich people became even richer _____ making others work for them _____.	☐
In den USA wurde diese Praxis 1865 abgeschafft: Der **Kongress verabschiedete** ein **Gesetz** zur Abschaffung der Sklaverei.	This was made illegal in the USA in 1865: _____ _____ an _____ abolishing slavery.	☐
Trotz dieses Gesetzes **befreiten** viele **Grundbesitzer** ihre Sklaven nicht.	_____ this law, many _____ didn't _____ their slaves.	☐
Viele Menschen, die sich mit den Sklaven **identifizierten**, **beschwerten sich** und kämpften für die **Sache**.	Many people who _____ with the slaves _____ and fought for the _____.	☐
Dies war der Beginn des Bürgerkrieges, in dem **Patrioten** aus dem Norden gegen die aus dem Süden kämpften.	This was the start of Civil War, where _____ from the North fought against those from the South.	☐
Dies war die Zeit, als viele Menschen **Aktivisten** wurden, weil sie es für **nötig** hielten zu handeln.	This was when many people became _____ because they thought it _____ to act.	☐

5 Jumbled words

Put the letters in the right order and write down the words.

1. SORGNESC _____
2. CANTIEN _____
3. RYAVLES _____
4. DEILMD SEAG _____
5. SCAVIITT _____
6. TATIROP _____

forty-three 43

4 Language 1

→ pages 70–72

What do you remember?

Das **Konzept** der Demokratie entstand in Griechenland, von wo aus es sich in der Welt **ausbreitete**.	The _____ of democracy comes from Greece, from where it _____ throughout the world.
Heutzutage sind alle Staaten **West**europas Demokratien.	Nowadays, all of the countries in _____ Europe are democracies.
Es gibt aber auch heute noch **Diktatoren**, die es nicht für wichtig halten, dass **Einzelpersonen wählen** können.	However, even today there are still _____ who don't think it's important for _____ to be able to _____ .
In einigen Gesellschaften hat die **Geheimpolizei** eine große Macht.	In some societies the _____ has a lot of power.
Viele Menschen **erhalten** nicht die Dinge, für die eine **Notwendigkeit** besteht.	Many people don't _____ the things they have a _____ for.
Für viele sind nicht einmal Kleidung und Nahrung **bezahlbar**.	For many, even clothes and food aren't _____ .
Ob jemand arm oder reich ist, ist **relativ**.	Whether someone is rich or poor is _____ .

6 Correct the mistake

A student has handed in his homework, but it is full of grammar mistakes. Help the teacher to correct them!

1. There is hard for teenagers to fight for rights.

   _____

2. There is not easy for governments to create more democracy.

   _____

3. It is important giving teens enough freedom.

   _____

4. It is wrong for politicians to taking away rights.

   _____

5. There are a need for journalists to report human rights problems.

   _____

Language 1 4

→ pages 70–72

What do you remember?

Oliver Twist ist die Geschichte eines Jungen, der den **Verlust** seiner Eltern erleiden musste und nach London geht.	Oliver Twist is the story of a boy who has suffered the _____ of his parents and goes to London.
Als er dort ankommt, trifft er Fagin, den Anführer einer Gruppe von Kindern. Er wird von Fagin für die gleiche Arbeit **rekrutiert**, die er und seine Gang machen: **Taschendiebstahl** in den Straßen Londons.	When he gets there, he meets Fagin, the leader of a group of kids. Fagin _____ Oliver to do the same job he and his gang do: _____ in the streets of London.
Zunächst **tut** Oliver **das gern**, aber dann ändert er seine Meinung und fühlt sich so schlecht, dass er nicht mehr in den _____ schauen kann.	At first, Oliver _____ this, but then he changes his mind and feels so bad about himself that he cannot look in the _____ .
Dies ist keine wahre Geschichte, doch das Gleiche geschieht noch heute mit **Rumänen**, die in verschiedene Länder **geschmuggelt** werden.	This isn't a true story, yet it still happens today, with _____ who are _____ into different countries.

7 Infinitive or gerund?

Put in the gerund or the infinitive form of the verbs in brackets. Then put the parts of the dialogue into the correct order by filling in the numbers 1–8.

- ⬤ We have _____ (be) there earlier. The march starts at 2 pm.

- ⬤ Yes, you're right. That makes me angry, too!

- ⬤ Hi Jessie. How are you? I want _____ (invite) you to the Gay Pride March.

- ⬤ Absolutely! How about _____ (meet) in town at 6 pm?

- ⬤ Haha! No, not at all. I'd like _____ (go) because gays and lesbians do not have the same rights as heterosexual people. People not _____ (be) treated equally makes me mad!

- ⬤ So I guess you want to come?

- ⬤ Hey Jenny. The Gay Pride March? Do you have _____ (be) gay _____ (go)?

- ⬤ Right, I'll meet you at 2 pm in front of the cinema.

4 Talkwise

→ page 73

What do you remember?

Gestern ging ich in mein Lieblingscafé, um dort meinen morgendlichen Kaffee zu trinken. Ganz ehrlich, das ist der beste Kaffee der Welt! Sie haben nicht nur den normalen, **alltäglichen** Kaffee, sondern alle möglichen Sorten und außerdem die frischesten **Zutaten**.	Yesterday I went to my favourite café to drink my morning coffee. Honestly, this is the best coffee in the world! They don't just have normal, _____ coffee there, but all different kinds, and also the freshest _____.
Wie auch immer, ich setzte mich hin und diese Frau zündete sich im Café eine Zigarette an. Ich reagiere sehr **empfindlich** auf Rauch.	Anyway, I sat down and this woman lit a cigarette inside the café. I'm very _____ to smoke.
Also sagte ich zu der Frau: „**Ich würde es begrüßen**, wenn Sie hier nicht rauchen würden."	So I said to the woman, "_____ you wouldn't smoke in here."
Sie antwortete mir: „Es ist nicht **angemessen**, dass Sie mich darum bitten, und außerdem sollte man eine **dickere** Haut haben."	She replied to me: "It is not _____ for you to ask me, and anyway, you should have a _____ skin."
Ich war schockiert! Ich finde, dass sie nicht gerade sehr **respektvoll** war.	I was shocked! I didn't think she was very _____ at all!
Wie auch immer, der Manager kam herüber und bat die Frau, das Café zu verlassen. Er war nicht sehr **tolerant** Menschen gegenüber, die das Gesetz ignorieren!	Anyway, the café manager came over and asked the woman to leave. He was not very _____ of people ignoring the law!

8 Pronunciation: The schwa

Underline the /ə/ sound in the words below. Then write down more words you know that have this sound and underline the /ə/ sound in those, too.

1. ingredients
2. appreciate
3. silent
4. secret
5. human
6. tolerant
7. appropriate
8. nature
9. holiday

_____

_____

_____

Language 2 | 4

→ pages 74/75

What do you remember?

Die Bürgerrechts**bewegung** in den USA wurde durch **Rassentrennung verursacht**.	The Civil Rights _____ in the USA was _____ by _____ .
Das heißt, dass Weiße und Schwarze in unterschiedliche Schulen gehen mussten und es den Schwarzen nicht erlaubt war, sich zu **integrieren**.	That is, whites and blacks had to go to different schools, and black people were not allowed to _____ .
Eines Tages hatte Rosa Parks, eine schwarze Frau, die genug hatte, großen **Mut**: Sie weigerte sich, ihren Sitzplatz im „weißen" Bereich eines Busses zu verlassen, obwohl sie von einer wütenden **Menschenmenge** angeschrien wurde.	One day, Rosa Parks, a black woman who had had enough, showed a lot of _____ : She refused to move from her seat in the white part of a bus even though a _____ of angry people were shouting at her.
Rosa Parks wurde zum **Vorbild** und **lenkte die Aufmerksamkeit der Menschen auf** das Problem des **Rassismus** in den USA.	Rosa Parks became a _____ and _____ the problem of _____ in the USA.

9 Cryptogram

Every number stands for a letter. The same numbers mean the same letters. Try to find all of the words. There is one word at the beginning to help you.

beginning word:

C	O	U	R	A	G	E
6	11	3	8	13	5	1

E	U		G	C		R				O		A			
1	2	3	4	5	6	7	8	9	10	11	12	13	14	15	16

1. ___ ___ ___ ___ ___ ___ ___ ___ ___ ___
   12 1 5 8 1 5 13 2 4 11 7

2. ___ ___ ___ ___ ___
   8 13 6 4 12 10

3. ___ ___ ___ ___ ___ ___ ___
   10 11 9 1 10 1 7 2

4. ___ ___ ___ ___ ___ ___ ___ ___
   8 11 14 1 10 11 16 1 14

5. ___ ___ ___ ___ ___ ___ ___ ___ ___
   4 7 2 1 5 8 13 2 1

6. ___ ___ ___ ___ ___ ___ ___
   6 11 7 6 1 15 2

7. ___ ___ ___ ___ ___ ___ ___ ___
   6 11 7 5 8 1 12 12

8. ___ ___ ___ ___ ___ ___ ___
   15 8 11 2 1 12 2

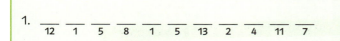

4 Language 2

→ pages 74/75

What do you remember?

Ich habe gestern Abend einen traurigen Film gesehen, der in einer **normalen** Schule spielte.	I saw a sad movie last night, which was set in an _____ school.
Darin ging es um eine Gruppe von Jungen, die einen ausländischen Schüler **mobbten**.	There was a group of boys who _____ a foreign student.
Sie **beschimpften** ihn, weil er mit den Füßen **schlurfte**.	They _____ because he _____ his feet.
Ein **Beobachter**, ein Mädchen aus der Klasse des Jungen, sah das Mobbing mit an, doch sie war **still** und **äußerte sich** nicht **dazu**.	An _____, a girl in the boy's class, watched the bullying, but she was _____ and didn't _____.
Es war die **Hölle** für den ausländischen Jungen, denn die Gang wartete immer an der Ecke seines **Blocks** und ließ ihn in den Schulfluren nicht **vorbeigehen**.	It was _____ for the boy as the gang was always waiting on the corner of his _____ and wouldn't let him _____ in the school corridors.
Letztendlich war der Junge so **verängstigt**, dass er eines der Gangmitglieder **umbrachte** und ins Gefängnis gehen musste.	In the end, the boy was so _____ that he _____ one of the gang members and had to go to prison.
Wenn jemand etwas gegen das Mobbing getan hätte, hätte das bestimmt das Leben des Jungen **verändert**.	If someone had done something about the bullying, it would probably have _____ to the boy's life.

10 Gerund or infinitive?

Match the beginnings with the endings to make correct sentences.

1. Not getting any birthday presents
2. It is crazy
3. It is polite
4. Listening to your teacher
5. It's disappointing
6. Going outside in a T-shirt in December

- to go outside in a T-shirt in December.
- is crazy.
- not to get any birthday presents.
- is disappointing.
- to listen to your teacher.
- is polite.

48 forty-eight

Language 2 — 4

→ pages 74/75

What do you remember?

	People sit on _____ in the park to relax.
Die **Integration** in eine neue Gesellschaft ist nicht immer einfach.	_____ into a new society isn't always easy.
	I bought this _____ when I was on holiday.
Ein **Ausbeuterbetrieb** ist eine kleine Fabrik mit sehr schlechten Arbeitsbedingungen.	A _____ is a small factory with very bad working conditions.
Wir müssen stark sein, um diese schlimme Zeit zu **überstehen**.	We must be strong to _____ this bad time.
Ich bin **begierig** darauf, meine Fahrprüfung morgen zu bestehen.	I'm _____ to pass my driving test tomorrow.
Wenn du einen Job nicht **richtig** machst, ist er nicht wert, getan zu werden.	If you don't do a job _____, it's not worth doing at all.
Es ist traurig, wenn Menschen nur **nach ihrem Aussehen beurteilt werden**.	It's very sad when people are only _____ by their _____!

11 Crossword puzzle

Look at the definitions and write down the right words. The letters in green give you the solution.

1. a factory you often find in poor countries
2. When you really want to do something, you are …
3. the opposite of heaven
4. someone others can look up to
5. another word for normal
6. someone who watches something carefully
7. a piece of furniture you can sit on in a park
8. another word for really scared

Solution: _____ !

4 Writing texts

→ page 77

What do you remember?

Dschingis Khan ist ein berühmtes Beispiel für einen **Tyrannen**.	Genghis Khan is a famous example of a _____.
Diese Landschaft **weist** viele Seen und Flüsse **auf**.	This landscape _____ lots of lakes and rivers.
Ich habe nicht genug **Material**, um das Projekt zu beenden.	I don't have enough _____ to finish the project.
Der Ganges **fließt** durch Indien.	The Ganges _____ through India.
Bei der Bewerbung um einen Job sind gute **Referenzen** sehr wichtig.	When you apply for a job, good _____ are very important.
Sein Charakter ist sehr **eindimensional**.	His character is very _____.
Im Moment ist mein **Verstand** voller verschiedener Dinge.	I've got a lot on my _____ at the moment.
Zuerst sagt er, dass er mich liebt, dann sagt er, dass er mich hasst. Was für ein **Widerspruch**! Ich mag ihn **jedoch** trotzdem. Der **Gedanke** an ihn bringt mich immer zum Lächeln.	First he says he loves me, then he says he hates me. What a _____ ! I still like him, _____ . The _____ of him always makes me smile.
„**Historisch**" bedeutet, dass etwas Teil der Geschichte ist.	'_____' means that it's part of history.
Ich mag in meinem Zuhause eine **friedliche** Atmosphäre.	I like a _____ atmosphere in my home.

12 Dialogue

Put the parts of the dialogue into the correct order by filling in the numbers 1–7.

_____ **A** Sam: That sounds like a contradiction to me!

_____ **B** Sam: Which one?

_____ **C** Jenny: Well, tyrants are often seen as one-dimensional characters. They were known for their reign of terror, but actually, they were quite peaceful people.

_____ **D** Jenny: Yes, it does. I have to find out more about the topic.

_____ **E** Jenny: The one about tyrants. I need to check a reference.

_____ **F** Jenny: Have you got that history book?

_____ **G** Sam: Here you are. What are you checking?

Writing texts 4

→ page 77

What do you remember?

Wenn jemand **obdachlos** ist, hat er keinen Platz zum Wohnen.	If someone is _____, they don't have anywhere to live.	☐
Ein teures Auto kann ein **Statussymbol** sein.	An expensive car can be a _____.	☐
Wenn man nicht zur Schule geht, ist man **ungebildet**.	If you don't go to school, you are _____.	☐
Bitte sei leise, ich versuche mich **auf** meine Arbeit zu **konzentrieren**.	Please be quiet, I'm trying to _____ my work.	☐
Yoga ist sehr gut für den Körper und die **Seele**.	Yoga is excellent for the body and the _____.	☐
Ich hoffe, mein Ziel zu **erreichen**, Anwalt zu werden.	I hope to _____ my goal of becoming a lawyer.	☐
Biographisches Schreiben ist, wenn man über das Leben einer Person schreibt.	_____ writing is when you write about someone's life.	☐
Wenn Sie **weitere** Details benötigen, mailen Sie mir bitte.	If you'd like _____ details, please e-mail me.	☐
„**Bio**" ist die Kurzform von „Biographie".	'_____' is the short form of 'biography'.	☐
Ein **Gewand** ist ein langes **Kleidungs**stück.	A _____ is a long piece of _____.	☐

13 Word building

Draw lines to the right suffix to make nouns or adjectives. Add other words you know to the boxes.

1. cloth
2. uneducat
3. home
4. peace
5. integrat
6. historic

Suffixes: -ion, -less, -al, -ing, -ful, -ed

Boxes: -ion | -less | -al | -ing | -ful | -ed

4 Text

→ pages 78–80

What do you remember?

ewig • Tod	Nobody can live _____, _____ is part of life.
verbieten	Women are _____ from driving in Saudi Arabia.
idealistisch	It's _____ to think you can change the whole world.
vorgeben	Why _____ to be something you are not?
Gerücht	There's a _____ going around that Lady Gaga is going to have a baby.
unausstehlich	That boy is so _____ – he doesn't listen to his mother at all.
emotional	My friend cries all the time – he is so _____.
poetisch	The e-mail he sent me was very _____.
harmonisch	We never argue. Our relationship is very _____.
dissonant, nicht harmonierend	He loves listening to Death Metal. To me, it sounds ugly and _____.

14 Word families

The following nouns are new to you, but you already know an adjective from the same word family. Write down the adjective and try to guess the meaning of the noun.

Noun	Adjective	Meaning
emotion		
dissonance		
idealism		
harmony		
poetry		
obnoxiousness		

Text 4

→ pages 78–80

What do you remember?	
jmdn. beschäftigen	This great new song has been _____ since I heard it on the radio this morning.
Liedtext • Refrain	The _____ were awesome and it had an amazing _____, but the song is quite controversial.
allgemein • Botschaft • beleidigen	Some people say that the _____ _____ of the song _____ them.
Beliebtheit • Ziel • einen Zugang zu etw. finden	The song's _____ has increased with its _____ market – teenagers who like listening to music they can _____ on a personal level.
üblich	It is very _____ that adults and teenagers don't like the same type of music.

15 Lyrics analysis

Read part of the lyrics of a protest song below. Say what the message and style of the lyrics is and use two adjectives to describe them.

Dear Mr. President,
Come take a walk with me.
Let's pretend we're just two people and
You're not better than me.
I'd like to ask you some questions if we can speak honestly.

What do you feel when you see all the homeless on the street?
Who do you pray for at night before you go to sleep?
What do you feel when you look in the mirror?
Are you proud?
(Pink, "Dear Mr. President")

Message: _____

_____

Style: _____

Adjectives: _____

fifty-three 53

4 Text

→ pages 78–80

What do you remember?

zeitlos	Everyone likes to think that their taste in music is _____.
veraltet	But often both young people and adults think the others' music sounds very _____!
Doppelmoral	I think it's a _____ when people who swear complain that they don't like songs that use bad language.
Lösung • umgehen mit • speziell	The best _____ would be for people to wear headphones, so if people can't _____ a _____ kind of music, they don't have to.

16 Word match

Read the statements on the left and draw lines to match them with the right adjectives.

1. This song makes me feel happy and sad.
2. This song reminds me of Goethe's work.
3. I feel really relaxed when I hear this song.
4. The music and the lyrics sound wonderful.
5. The harmony is really awful.
6. This song could be from any time.
7. The song has a message: It wants to tell people that they can change the world if they really want to.
8. This song is clearly from last year.

a) dissonant
b) harmonious
c) emotional
d) peaceful
e) poetic
f) idealistic
g) dated
h) timeless

17 Protest songs: Your opinion

Which modern protest songs do you know? Do you like them? Why or why not? Think about the artists, the lyrics, the music …

_____
_____
_____
_____

18 A quiz

Try to guess the meaning of these colloquial expressions. Tip: The pictures on the right might help you.

1. If someone is getting on your nerves, they are …
   - [ ] a) annoying you.
   - [ ] b) helping you.
   - [ ] c) doing your homework.
   - [ ] d) hurting you.

2. Big-time means …
   - [ ] a) a long time.
   - [ ] b) a lot.
   - [ ] c) a big break.
   - [ ] d) a delicious meal.

3. If someone is in your face they are being …
   - [ ] a) romantic.
   - [ ] b) aggressive.
   - [ ] c) relaxed.
   - [ ] d) tired.

4. Your friend says his teacher went ballistic. The teacher is …
   - [ ] a) really happy.
   - [ ] b) extremely nervous.
   - [ ] c) overweight.
   - [ ] d) very angry.

19 Choose the correct option

Underline the right word to complete the sentences.

1. I couldn't go to school because of my (**sick** • **sickness**).
2. The soldier was given a medal for his (**brave** • **bravery**).
3. (**Homelessness** • **homeless**) is a problem all over the world.
4. Some movie stars hate being (**fame** • **famous**).
5. That guy is really (**intolerant** • **intolerance**) of foreign people.
6. I think (**young** • **youth**) people have more problems today.

4 Check-out

20 Tolerance and respect

What would you say in the following situations? Try to be as polite as possible.

21 Word search

Find ten words in the box. The words go → and ↓.

M	I	M	O	E	Q	U	A	L	I	T	Y	A	A	G	J	C	P
U	P	D	S	E	G	R	E	G	A	T	I	O	N	A	S	C	E
R	S	B	D	W	S	E	U	T	M	O	C	D	R	H	I	H	A
D	S	L	N	O	T	L	Y	B	Y	L	R	Z	S	Z	S	X	C
E	Q	O	F	X	J	I	B	P	O	E	T	I	C	S	Z	G	E
R	A	C	I	S	T	G	J	P	C	R	Y	Q	P	J	W	D	F
L	R	K	H	E	X	I	M	L	I	A	L	Y	R	I	C	S	U
W	D	M	P	F	P	O	H	U	H	N	I	G	K	C	T	J	L
C	V	A	U	I	K	N	T	Y	T	T	N	V	N	J	S	S	G

22 Word match

Match a word from the first box with a word from the second box to make words from Unit 3.

Middle • child • racial • equal • secret • speak • double • one-

equality • Ages • out • police • rights • standard • dimensional • labour

1. _____
2. _____
3. _____
4. _____
5. _____
6. _____
7. _____
8. _____

Revision Unit 3 + 4

1 Word stress

How are these words from Unit 3 and Unit 4 pronounced? Complete the grid.

dignity, shampoo, direction, regime, carpet, ingredient, democracy, equal, effect, slavery, protest, dictator, importance, relationship, lesbian

● ●	● ●	● ● ●	● ● ●	● ● ● ●

2 Jumbled words

Put the letters in the right order to complete the sentences.

1. When two people love each other, they often get _____. DIMARRE
2. You use this to clean your hair. _____ POOAMHS
3. When people disagree and are angry, they sometimes do this. _____ GUEAR
4. a crime when people steal from people in the street _____ CKIP-KEPOCINGT
5. Many people like to watch this at home. _____ VIEETLSONI
6. another word for very scared _____ RRETIDEFI
7. There are three famous ones in Egypt. _____ MIDYRAP
8. the story of someone's life _____ GRPHAYIOB

3 Word classes

Write down words you know from Unit 3 and Unit 4 under these headings.

Adjective	Verb	Noun	Conjunction

Zoom-in

What do you remember?
continent – unique • roo – kangaroo • Koalas – platypi – down under • Aborigines – minority – society • indigenous • outback • separated – Aboriginal • forced – relocation

1 Mixed bag
1. outback • indigenous • Aborigines
2. Aboriginal • forced relocation
3. continent • separated • unique • Kangaroos • koalas

What do you remember?
Aussies – G'day – Good day • endlessness – rainforest • ozone layer – destroyed • skin cancer • Forests – tundra – Canadian • monarch – head of state • portrait

2 Landscapes
1. tundra 2. outback 3. desert 4. forest
5. rainforest 6. beach
Solution: Aussie

What do you remember?
dominating – status • systematic – regulation • foreign • influence • pop culture • superpower • led

3 English words in German
Lösungsvorschlag:
computer, receiver, sweatshirt, jeans, sandwich

4 Your opinion
Individuelle S-Lösungen

What do you remember?
dialects • democracy • possibility • elections – civil rights • cancer • Poverty – Indian • broke up – independence • relations

5 Find the missing word
1. Aussie 2. Aborigines 3. Australia 4. dialect
5. continent

6 Spot the mistakes
1. Free elections and **civil** rights are part of a **democracy**.
2. Australia is also called '**down under**' and '**G'day**' is an Australian way to say 'hello'.

What do you remember?
dish • survey – president • torn apart • Hindi • settlement – sq. – square • Namáste – Howzit • reminder • Bollywood

7 Word formation
2. society 3. Canadian 4. endless 5. settlement
6. to remind 7. regulation 8. to lead 9. possibility
10. poor

8 Bits and pieces
forest, tundra, declare, outback, cancer, status, survey, portrait

What do you remember?
order • crowded • banker – called in • leader • record • Apartheid – racist – system • separateness – blacks • police state • townships • middle class – wealth

9 Jumbled words
India: Hindi, Bollywood
Canada: tundra, French
South Africa: Howzit, apartheid, township
Australia: outback, Aboriginal, roo

Lösungen

Unit 1

What do you remember?
characterization • breath • confident – direct • adapted – abridged

1 Aboriginal life
Lösungsvorschlag:
1. The Australian outback is huge and seems endless.
2. Many Aboriginal families were torn apart by forced relocation.
3. The Aborigines have a unique culture.
4. The Aborigines are a minority in Australian culture.
5. It's sad that there are so many separated Aboriginal families.

2 Describing a character
1. helpful 2. aggressive 3. direct 4. confident
5. racist

What do you remember?
point of view • World Heritage Site • shorthand • interest • glass-bottom

3 Word search

1. survey 2. characterization 3. shorthand
4. Apartheid 5. record 6. breath 7. dominated
8. wealth 9. abridged 10. dish

What do you remember?
posted • Oz • barbie – barbecue – rooftop terrace • all kinds of – exotic • made – emu – yummy • crocodile • witchetty grubs – green ants • preconceptions

4 Say it in a different way
1. dishes 2. characterization 3. Post 4. made
5. crowded 6. Aborigines

What do you remember?
used to – penal colony • Convicts • coat of arms • shipload – delivered • bit of information – Asian-Pacific • have my car repaired • nearby • version – aspect • ancestors – criminal • first-time – consulate • Let me – form

5 Odd word out
1. 'Ancestor' doesn't fit in because it doesn't have to do with crime.
2. 'Elephant' doesn't fit in because it doesn't live in Australia.
3. 'G'day' doesn't fit in because it isn't a name for Australia.
4. 'Survey' doesn't fit in because it isn't a landscape.

What do you remember?
road trip • return • perspective • turning point • hint • worry-wart • Peer editing • climax • princess-like • foreshadowing – red-herrings

6 Matching
1 d) 2 f) 3 g) 4 a) 5 h) 6 c) 7 e) 8 b)

What do you remember?
is supposed to be • formal • is said to be

7 Peter's blog
Aussies • G'day • down under • outback • rainforest • kangaroos • exotic • worry-wart • skin cancer • destroyed • ozone layer

used to • penal colony • interested • convicts • barbie • all kinds of • dishes • crocodile • made • green ants • posted • climax • Aboriginal • aspect

8 A crossword
Across:
1. foreshadowing 3. separated 5. shorthand
7. consulate 8. cancer 9. democracy 12. foreign
13. adapted 14. indigenous 15. banker

Down:
2. superpower 4. election 5. shipload 6. monarch
10. abridged 11. nearby

Unit 2

What do you remember?
career • GCSE – General Certificate of Secondary Education – study • A-levels • exams • work experience – nurse • social work – higher education • architect • foreign languages

1 Jumbled words
GCSE • A-levels • higher education • architect • career • exams • study • social work • nurse

What do you remember?
took – exam • suit • dead bodies • opportunity – musician • reaches – competitive • lawyer • reliable • questionnaire

2 Verbs and their friends
to take: an exam, A-levels, GCSEs
to study: Maths, foreign languages, Science
to reach: the age of 18, wealth
to become: a lawyer, an architect, a nurse, famous

3 Spot the mistakes
1. Let's complete the **questionnaire** for the survey on **career** wishes.
2. After the **GCSEs** Sue went on to **higher education**.

What do you remember?
stereotypes • bank • practical • construction • personnel manager – tactful • railway system • technical

4 Synonyms
1. career 2. exam 3. opportunity

5 Word search

P	V	F	S	T	E	R	E	O	T	Y	P	E	W	P
R	R	U	T	R	E	A	E	T	Z	U	C	A	B	M
A	A	Q	U	E	S	T	I	O	N	N	A	I	R	E
C	A	L	D	L	Y	A	A	S	R	U	R	I	V	A
T	T	M	Y	I	R	E	N	U	R	S	E	Y	H	K
I	U	B	V	A	A	R	C	H	I	T	E	C	T	U
C	O	O	U	B	A	N	K	C	G	O	R	V	N	T
A	P	U	O	L	I	O	S	R	U	O	N	O	O	R
L	K	T	T	E	C	H	N	I	C	A	L	O	P	B

What do you remember?
university • whiz-kid • adviser – image • pay – work my way up • deadline • support service

6 Say it in a different way
1. pay 2. suit 3. deadline 4. image

7 What about you?
Individuelle S-Lösungen

What do you remember?
leaflet – + – plus • employ – hairdresser • mainly • meet a deadline • put me off • quality • multimedia – competition • to rise

8 Word formation
1. pay 2. practical 3. musician 4. mainly
5. competitive 6. banker 7. questionnaire 8. lawyer

9 Mixed bag
1. put me off 2. qualities 3. whiz-kid

What do you remember?
date of birth • knowledge • volunteer • Architecture • letters of application • enclose – CV – Curriculum Vitae – reference • application – placement • available • apply for • print – signature • Yours sincerely • encl.

10 Style
Lösungsvorschlag:
I'm writing to apply for the job as a hairdresser. Your name was given to me by a friend of mine. I've been cutting my friends' and family's hair for years, so I already have some knowledge of the job. I have good social and communication skills, so dealing with customers wouldn't be a problem …

What do you remember?
fluent • meteorologist – predicted • weather forecast • direction • appointment • Meteorology • waiting room

11 Career crossword
Lösungsvorschlag:
Across:
1. someone who plays a musical instrument
3. someone who works in a bank
5. someone who helps people who have problems with the law
6. someone who works in a school

Down:
1. someone who predicts the weather
2. someone who cuts people's hair
4. someone who works in a hospital and helps doctors

What do you remember?
has her head in the clouds • Just you wait • decided on • whatsit • stupid • served • work out • hot • verbs of perception

12 Find the missing word
1. meteorologist 2. meteorology 3. to rise 4. nurse
5. direction 6. to study

13 Verbs
Lösungsvorschlag:
phrasal verbs: to decide on, to work out, to go on, to think of
verbs of perception: to see, to feel, to hear, to taste
irregular verbs: to write, to break, to take, to be

What do you remember?
was interviewed for a job • made a bad impression • body language • interviewer • impression – applicant • suitable • employer

14 Correct the sentences
1. ~~bad~~ good 2. ~~employer~~ applicant 3. ~~website~~ signature 4. ~~living room~~ waiting room 5. ~~friends~~ deadlines

15 Bits and pieces
direction, volunteer, technical, signature, construction, quality, employer, musician

What do you remember?
paper • pass – exam • gardener – builder – politician • part-time • be affected • Would you believe it – childhood • made up

16 A job interview
After the GCSE exams I did social work and a work experience in a hospital. • Medicine has always interested me and I like practical work. • I think I'm reliable and good at dealing with people.

What do you remember?
turned – 'm off • upside-down • tent – grabbed • in the middle of – thrown around • get his act together • trailer

17 How does the text say it?
1. upside-down 2. is grabbed 3. affected 4. making it up

18 Jumbled words
1. tent 2. builder 3. trailer 4. childhood
5. politician 6. gardener

What do you remember?
African – cured – diseases – drugs • campaign – begging for – medicine – suffered • sticks • collaborative • It's up to you – wallets • gift

19 Words and pictures
1. wallet 2. trailer 3. builder 4. tent

20 Mixed bag
1. part-time 2. made • up 3. in the middle of
4. is • affected 5. wallet

What do you remember?
suffixes • 's likely to • 's certain to

21 Word families
Lösungsvorschlag:
1. **musician:** music, musical
2. **unhappy:** happy, happiness
3. **employment:** to employ sb, employer
4. **training:** to train sb, trainer

22 Sally's first interview
Lösungsvorschlag:
1. She should make sure that she's in the right place by the right time.
2. She should wait until she is asked to take a seat.
3. She should feel fresh on the day, have answers ready to give at the interview and answer questions with more than 'yes' or 'no'.
4. She should ask important questions about the job and show that she's really interested in the company.

What do you remember?
advert • workplace • adverbial clause

23 Word parts
1. predicts 2. childhood 3. applicant • impression
4. application • employer 5. diseases 6. appointment • lawyer 7. volunteer 8. campaign 9. fluent • foreign
10. career • suitable 11. musician 12. trailer

Revision Unit 1 + 2
1 Australia
Individuelle S-Lösungen

2 Your interview
Individuelle S-Lösungen

Unit 3

What do you remember?
covered • comfortable • prove • Go ahead • directly • roaring • feel comfortable

1 Jumbled words
1. prove   2. comfortable   3. directly   4. Cover   5. Go ahead   6. roaring

2 One letter – different sounds

[ʌ]	[uː]
cover, comfortable, money, love	prove, lose, move, two

What do you remember?
power • tracks • television • media-mad

3 Media crossword
1. power   2. entertainment   3. advertisements   4. programme   5. films   6. television   7. media-mad   8. tracks

What do you remember?
gossip • Social networking sites • of no importance • get married • argue • are seeing • 'm unable to • In no way • brain • teletext • brain power • These days • in reply to

4 Odd one out
1. study   2. split up   3. Of course!   4. in the past

What do you remember?
spoken – written • summarize • view • Filter • multi-tasking • issues • effect • hardly • shampoo • source

5 Mixed bag: The presentation
issue • filter • Summarize • spoken/written • spoken/written • source • effect • view

What do you remember?
brackets • normal type • italics • wide shot • close-up • soft lighting • romantic • zoom in • shot • directions • medium shot

6 Word fields
Camera work: zoom-in, medium shot, soft lighting, close-up, wide shot
Script writing: brackets, normal type, italics, catch phrase, directions

What do you remember?
shrugging • sucking • mad with • make a choice • turn away from me • catch phrase • instead of • voice-over • mad about

7 Spot the mistake
1. ~~of~~ with   2. ~~at~~ in   3. ~~off~~ up   4. ~~to~~ from   5. ~~in~~ of   6. ~~out~~ for   7. ~~of~~ about   8. ~~on~~ about

What do you remember?
because of • cause • tied up • therefore • as • local • since • busks

8 Sentence matching
1. The cause of my headache was too much sun.
2. I got a headache because the sun was too hot.
3. Can you help me as you're so good at Maths?
4. Can you help me so I can finish this quickly?
5. The car broke down because it was so old.
6. The car broke down, therefore we were late.
7. She missed the party because of her exam.
8. She missed the party because she was ill.

What do you remember?
appears • from now • viewers

9 Word search: The media

R	O	M	T	N	E	M	N	I	A	T	R	E	T	N	E	P	B	L	M	N
E	N	X	E	S	M	Y	O	W	U	G	L	U	C	X	Q	H	Z	Y	R	O
P	K	I	L	D	C	A	M	E	R	A	S	H	O	T	U	N	O	A	Y	I
A	D	V	E	R	T	I	S	E	M	E	N	T	I	V	A	W	O	X	Z	T
P	P	G	T	U	D	S	P	O	H	Y	B	M	J	W	X	R	M	O	N	C
S	X	R	E	V	O	E	C	I	O	V	Y	L	I	G	H	T	I	N	G	E
W	Y	D	X	P	D	I	H	P	R	C	C	X	U	L	A	T	N	Q	P	R
E	A	J	T	E	L	E	V	I	S	I	O	N	B	O	Z	C	F	P	G	I
N	P	L	F	J	G	F	I	D	O	F	U	F	X	E	Q	D	X	I	M	D

entertainment, camera shot, advertisement, voice-over, lighting, television, newspaper, teletext, zoom-in, direction

10 Definitions
1. shot   2. viewer   3. issue   4. script   5. headline

Unit 4

What do you remember?
Human rights – tolerance • recent – states – qualify – democratic • Same-sex – relationships • gay – lesbian • parliament – position of power

1 Just for fun: Songs about human rights
Individuelle S-Lösungen

What do you remember?
rights • human • authoritarian – regimes • freedom of speech – religion – protest • equal • equal opportunities – democracies • dignity

2 Word stress

● ●	● ● ●	● ● ●	● ● ● ●
equal	parliament	religion	industrial
recent	tolerance	invention	especially
human	dignity	position	democracy
protest	lesbian	commercial	apologize

What do you remember?
Racial equality • brotherhood • developing world • proportion – males • positions • Labour • child labour • satisfactory

3 Matching
1. j) 2. i) 3. a) 4. b) 5. c) 6. d) 7. h) 8. f)
9. e) 10. g)

What do you remember?
sex • tolerate • protest • represent • basis • spirit • least • considered to be • continuing

4 A quiz
1. parliament (Sweden)
2. regime (Iran, North Korea and Myanmar)
3. gay (Yes, it was one of the first countries in the world to allow same-sex relationships.)
4. democracy (Greece)
5. developing (China, India and Brazil)

What do you remember?
slavery • Middle Ages – slaves • ancient – pyramids • by – by force • Congress – passed – act • In spite of – landowners – free • identified – complained – cause • patriots • activists – necessary

5 Jumbled words
1. congress 2. ancient 3. slavery 4. Middle Ages
5. activist 6. patriot

What do you remember?
concept – spread • Western • dictators – individuals – vote • secret police • receive – need • affordable • relative

6 Correct the mistake
1. **It's** hard for teenagers to fight for **their** rights.
2. **It isn't** easy for governments to create more democracy.
3. It is important **to give** teens enough freedom.
4. It is wrong for politicians **to take away** rights.
5. **There is** a need for journalists to report human rights problems.

What do you remember?
loss • recruits – pick-pocketing • is happy to do – mirror • Romanians – smuggled

7 Infinitive or gerund?
7 (to be), 4, 1 (to invite), 6 (meeting), 3 (to go • being), 5, 2 (to be • to go), 8

What do you remember?
everyday – ingredients • sensitive • I'd appreciate it if • appropriate – thicker • respectful • tolerant

8 Pronunciation: The schwa
1. ingred<u>ie</u>nts 2. appreci<u>a</u>te 3. sil<u>e</u>nt 4. secr<u>e</u>t
5. hum<u>a</u>n 6. toler<u>a</u>nt 7. appropri<u>a</u>te 8. nat<u>u</u>re
9. hol<u>i</u>day

What do you remember?
movement – caused – segregation • integrate • courage – mob • role model – brought people's attention to – racism

9 Cryptogram

E	T	U	I	G	C	N	R	V	M	O	S	A	L	P	D
1	2	3	4	5	6	7	8	9	10	11	12	13	14	15	16

1. segregation 2. racism 3. movement 4. role model
5. integrate 6. concept 7. congress 8. protest

What do you remember?
ordinary • bullied • called him names – shuffled • observer – silent – speak out • hell – block – pass • terrified – murdered • made a difference

10 Gerund or infinitive?
1. Not getting any birthday presents is disappointing.
2. It is crazy to go out in a T-shirt in December.
3. It is polite to listen to your teacher.
4. Listening to your teacher is polite.
5. It's disappointing not to get any birthday presents.
6. Going outside in a T-shirt in December is crazy.

What do you remember?
benches • Integration • carpet • sweatshop • get through • eager • properly • judged – appearance

11 Crossword puzzle
1. sweatshop 2. eager 3. hell 4. role model
5. ordinary 6. observer 7. bench 8. terrified

Solution: Well done!

What do you remember?
tyrant • features • material • flows • references • one-dimensional • mind • contradiction – though – thought • Historical • peaceful

12 Dialogue
1 F 2 B 3 E 4 G 5 C 6 A 7 D

What do you remember?
homeless • status symbol • uneducated • focus on • soul • achieve • Biographical • further • Bio • robe – clothing

13 Word buildung
1. clothing 2. uneducated 3. homeless 4. peaceful 5. integration 6. historical

What do you remember?
forever – death • banned • idealistic • pretend • rumor • obnoxious • emotional • poetic • harmonious • dissonant

14 Word families

Noun	Adjective	Meaning
emotion	emotional	Emotion
dissonance	dissonant	Dissonanz, Missklang
idealism	idealistic	Idealismus
harmony	harmonious	Harmonie
poetry	poetic	Poesie
obnoxiousness	obnoxious	Unausstehlichkeit

What do you remember?
on my mind • lyrics – refrain • general – message – offends • popularity – target – relate to • common

15 Lyrics analysis
Lösungsvorschlag:
Message: The singer wants to tell people that the president of the USA doesn't really care about people's problems and that he thinks he's better than them.
Style: The singer talks to the president on a personal level.
Adjectives: emotional, idealistic

What do you remember?
timeless • dated • double standard • solution – handle – specific

16 Word match
1. c) 2. e) 3. d) 4. b) 5. a) 6. h) 7. f) 8. g)

17 Protest songs: Your opinion
Individuelle S-Lösungen

18 A quiz
1. a) 2. b) 3. b) 4. d)

19 Choose the correct option
1. sickness 2. bravery 3. Homelessness 4. famous 5. intolerant 6. young

20 Tolerance and respect
Lösungsvorschlag:
1. Would you mind turning down your music a little?
2. Do you really think it's appropriate to laugh at those girls?
3. I'd appreciate it if you could be quieter so we can watch the movie.

21 Word search

M	I	M	O	E	Q	U	A	L	I	T	Y	A	A	G	J	C	P
U	P	D	S	E	G	R	E	G	A	T	I	O	N	A	S	C	E
R	S	B	D	W	S	E	U	T	M	O	C	D	R	H	I	H	A
D	S	L	N	O	T	L	Y	B	Y	L	R	Z	S	Z	S	X	C
E	Q	O	F	X	J	I	B	P	O	E	T	I	C	S	Z	G	E
R	A	C	I	S	T	G	J	P	C	R	Y	Q	P	J	W	D	F
L	R	K	H	E	X	I	M	L	I	A	L	Y	R	I	C	S	U
W	D	M	P	F	P	O	H	U	H	N	I	G	K	C	T	J	L
C	V	A	U	I	K	N	T	Y	T	T	N	V	N	J	S	S	G

22 Word match
1. Middle Ages 2. child labour 3. racial equality 4. equal rights 5. secret police 6. speak out 7. double standard 8. one-dimensional

Revision Unit 3 + 4
1 Word stress

• •	• •	• • •	• • •	• • • •
regime	equal	dictator	dignity	ingredient
effect	carpet	importance	slavery	democracy
shampoo	protest	direction	lesbian	relationship

2 Jumbled words
1. married 2. shampoo 3. argue 4. pick-pocketing 5. television 6. terrified 7. pyramid 8. biography

3 Word classes
Lösungsvorschlag:
Adjective: written, romantic, ancient, tolerant, poetic, idealistic
Verb: to prove, to protest, to represent, to ban, to offend, to vote
Noun: position, tolerance, dignity, direction, issue, power
Conjunction: instead of, as, since, therefore, in spite of